Music or Honesty

Music or Honesty

Rod Smith

Roof Books
New York

ISBN: 0-937804-07-X
Library of Congress Catalog Card No.: 2003092931

Versions of these poems have appeared in: *Articulate, B City, Bombay Gin, Cartografitti, Combo, Conundrum, The DC Poetry Anthology 1999-2000, The Hat, Ixnay, Lingo, The OASiA Broadside Series, Object, p.H, Primary Writing, Snare,* and *Tool: A Magazine. Abacus #104* comprised earlier versions of "Love Poems" and "On Weathering" as *The Lack* (*Love Poems, Targets, Flags*). "Ted's Head" appeared in the anthologies *100 Days*, edited by Andrea Brady and Keston Sutherland, and *Enough*, edited by Rick London and Leslie Scalapino.

Cover: *The Fall of Phaeton* (c.1605), Peter Paul Rubens, collection National Gallery of Art, Washington, D.C.

Roof Books are distributed by
Small Press Distribution
1341 Seventh Avenue
Berkeley, CA. 94710-1403.
Phone orders: 800-869-7553
www.spdbooks.org

 This book was made possible, in part, with public funds from the New York State Council on the Arts, a state agency.

NYSCA

ROOF BOOKS
are published by
Segue Foundation
303 East 8th Street
New York, NY 10009
www.roofbooks.com

CONTENTS

No Minus

the job

Skin II, 1973; Flags II, 1967-70; Flag on Orange Field;
The Critic Sees, 1962; Jubilee; Cicada, 1979; Untitled, 1977;
Dancers on a Plane, 1982; Tracing, 1978; Untitled, 1988;
Perilous Night, 1982; Study for Racing Thoughts, 1983;
Summer, 1985; Between the Clock and the Bed, 1982;
From False Start, 1960; Tracing, 1977

Some Haitian Proverbs

capsized bubbles scott-free & literary love back at the loping topoi

A heal, or example heard — how the rayed net soaks need. Remit
sentence in a flayed edition, mourning. Unstuck the, copped singular.
A stupid person is a real event.

       & How often
           or

            burning for folklore

                       — you there &
               in then, unaddressed— rolling
               the remembered miraculous pix
               up the story mocking the
               constitutive direct ornament's
                             mild
                moot softbuttoned lapidary
                How often it, clutched, remade
                the address to coddle
                Being in the furthering
                ABBREVIATED *bicyclette abreast* hopes
                from the hired car half-happy
                with raisinette wrappers &
                reeling in the cajoled bridge-incisor's
                nut-balm of a naked scrape's butter
                on it,

                unmercenary, slightly hungry,
                with the music very loud.

Limitations Are What We Are Outside Of

The look. West as was, special savings for preferred omicron lighting.

buoy— busting upward, delineated double-what when it crux and fed,
moping.

as for *mix which,*

clammy aggregates nap with memory's meteor shower of corporeal
semblance called
The one who gets
the best kept kempt battening
bidniss, the fall. a worried troll stalking
a strip mall. a line-up for cable theft. a borealic misfit
stuck in the stray nightshade of surgery, & sky.
& in need the worst lobe
scraps, settles back into bound proud glint-insist on all those copters'
adhered mist, highly
like a sex. Need as squirrel. & stand there, clumps, walk W whence the
combing netherfops make a good plummet ripen. trifocals seam us
—torquing the rubes

Everything Can Be Blamed On You

When you are poor

knot the forgotten graphic seedling. shores cup & plaster the
pasturizing prenuptial agreements.
a staff, maceing anagrams, stokes the unfulfilled discontinuous—
a kind of we-vapor.

"jesus was a sausage"

etc.

Sake

When you are poor, everything can be blamed on you.

no rope
                & string, no
snow's lace
              no
external peptic empire not-doing the not-doing—

         (no two colossal heads are alike)

          poems about seeing a bear
          outside your cabin
          don't really work for me

Beyond Mountains, More Mountains

The Book of Balance and Harmony says

> Because it is one word we think it represents one
> sort of activity.

Strike the prince with your spatula.

I think I feel safe up here. I think
> neurotic epiphanies blemish the reverting
> emptiness. I think

a clan point of going down wrong

willed the nix of she-spent lemons timing
out on the basis

> A MASKING OF THE REMAKE
> THEN, SO AS TO
> EXACERBATE TRANQUILITY
>
> A QUIET
> UNCOUTH
> SEALED AIR CORPORATION
>
> APPROXIMATELY 10 1/2 X 16
> INDETERMINATE UNITS USED
> PRIMARILY TO STUDY THE SPUTTER-

ING

> MINIMUM,
> THE FINAL STELLAR MASS
> EPIC AND ASSOCIATED REMNANTS
> IN NAKED TERMINAL OVERLAPS
> LIKE REPRINTS OF

PRESSED FEATURES
CREATED BY DEPRESSIONS
THEIR VOICES

(VIDEO WOMBATS)

INVENT TOMATOES

"SQUEEZE THE EAGLE CLUB!"

THE PREBIOTIC SOUP

IT IS FINISHED IN BEAUTY

Bootleg

In a debatable tureen, in nodal space, 37 squirrels, childishly igno-
rant of science, storm the gates of St. Mark's Place.

> Hot, hot pease, hot, hot, hot
> Hot are my pease, hot

The Wavers

commercials about seeing a bear
outside your cabin
work really well I think

Degradation's smattered imaginary
the realization of Thusness
flowing forth

paint is not food.

"but our job to build light"

Out the window in the hubbub dining   tune
axial to the coming warp-survive, & smelling clumps. ABAB, bad
slough forgetting censure in the overcomed road morphing nets.
an unequal regret & looky-here-structured summer months
cropfed *distingues* koalabies
       koalabies bent in the phone of the lorrie, basically
       funkin' — top the stand ornery, & stand there, shiny.

Sweet Sweet Sweet Sweet Sweet Dirt. Susie Asado.

a collaboration with Tom Raworth on possible future titles of
books by Anselm Berrigan.
Having written *They Beat Me Over the Head with a Sack* Anslem may
now wish to write:
My Head. The Sack. Continuous Contact.
The Countless Inexhaustible Manifestations of the Sacks We Have
Now I've *Got the Sack Motherfucker*
Oh, & All This Time I Thought It Was a Sack
etc.

The around write not so hush derivatives in the o my more stymied

de duro acento romano at the round
stilled
at the oppose
told.
Missouri born, penicillin bread, &
died instead
to march to the middlebrow beat
and one can, if one can
soaking in the mandala
warm colors
warm, casual colors
warm, ridiculous, casual colors
warm, moist, ridiculous casual colors
warm, alienated, moist ridiculous casual colors
warm & turned stolen license the terrible come near
& within fulfillment & change the wet wet mandalas
sharp point a shared exchange
unpleaseable brevity's profoundly hyperbolic negate dwindling

& warm

plummet

dwindling

the false instead at the round
stilled delete

hovering
—a genre's loved

numbering,
—Claraudient puffins

glittering in the infinite   understood   oblivion

Title

Anastasia found
herself going thwack
In the pert circumnambular weather — stuff wake ream in the
plead w/a flammable
nodding — the term _firing process_
something, & by what in that way we hold
Understood oblivion's presupposed
Hazel Equilibrium
Ipso factoid crossing the creek
To be given this written on the back
Of a matchbook when what you needed,
Like Kandinsky, was a gun.

Oppen at Altamont

against existence — the reactionary clique — the critical horizon
— comma — The stop that
ashen turns or "entails" street lit
due dissolving
the legal definition of mind—

ever-cloaked coloratura
choreographed on the flint—

    The day that I left Tibet they gave me this pig.

    umbrella
    desperately
    inner./
        ornithologically

                          emboldened cuts
                clover the
          denuding
                 plummet
              &

    describe Americoo inamorta

    the emotional economy

    the issue of the form of strife

    — fumes of seeing monstrous
    goons— carrying daisies the rest a rake
    stamped — shallow blaze of
                       — drop
    the dedication page, repencil
    the staving off

Disgusted Optimistic Lyric Language Poem

The dog has four paws, but it can only go in one direction. The wall's out of the bag. & the trail of tears, now stars, now aspirin . . . Time & reflection kill passion. Passion is power. Give that leg a bone.

inadvertent demobbed syllabic torturings (fried lichen nudists) still awkward about awareness[2] – time lights egged fluff faults chasing, are alive, are awaiting banking. problems.

But Mommy It Doesn't Have Confidence It's Not Alive

acoustic shadows

the melting material light

viscous

bovine

dissidence—

This movement is the restorative mention in the making of this
body which is this, the brief house of each moment. A reflection
can grow up & through & flash the tine of that which resides in
this, a or the or my, body. A sign says it is changed. toxic stubble.
abyss for a penny. here's an urchin. The impertinent decay is not
bound up with questions of identity. One is isn't. here's another
urchin. The impertinent decay is not bound up with questions of
identity. Hornfish, is it freezing with that snake tied to your fat
ass? Must get to hospital, can't die here. A ventricle enters the
moot ink, it is your lattice attracted to incommunicado— a moody
bedpost, tactless, in the toy decision. Orbit enters window palate.
Econometric Applications of Maximum Likelihood Methodology.
Flame of open further and kill. The kind of thing that might
move some old hippie to open a beerjoint called "Antinomy's."
clasp the funnel of flame. other days. other lovely grey walls across
the way. healing is a kind of ungrounded expectation, a sapphic
needle & mead, lux of wax corpuscles dating the mood-candy.
other days. other lovely grey walls across the way. peppermint
boyfriendology *burned all night* — refeed refood, making up with
clover. a blemish on the peripheral buddha you worry 'bout. a
specific kind of aleatoric aftertaste dramatizing the tendentious
barrelhousing intellectual commons— expenditure *cuts*. One is
isn't. When they want to kill a dog they say it's crazy. as one fries,
so one cooks. this relates to the tongue on things. Promote

wholesome devoted non-deludedness. this relates to the tongue on things. Obviously they have chosen to live that wall. this relates to the thing on things. Touches of going that through & across from it, a liquored skylick inside her dying movie reminisce. The chivalrous indecency iota. The act on aces the ordained orgone. Its mercurial torpor besmooched with tangent. These & the liquidity of tolerance; (Subsaharan) — coagulate inside momentous insistent foster argument.

Autopsy Turvy

"In 2000, we spent $281 billion on our militaty, which was more than the next 11 nations combined. By 2003, our expenditures will have risen to $378 billion. In other words, the *increase* in our defense budget from 1999-2003 will be more than the total amount spent annually by China, our next largest competitor."

— Jay Bookman, *The Atlanta Journal-Constitution*, 9/29/02

Ted's Head

So there's this episode of Mary Tyler Moore where Ted's trying to get a raise & after finagling and shenaniganizing he puts one over on Lou & gets his contract changed to non-exclusive so's he can do commercials which is not cool w/ Lou & the gang because Ted's just a brainless gimp & it hurts the image of the news to have the anchorman selling tomato slicers & dogfood so Lou gets despondent because the contract can't be rescinded but then he gets mad & calls Ted into his office & says, you know his voice, "You're going to stop doing commercials, Ted" & Ted says "why would I do that Lou?" & Lou says "Because if you don't I'll punch your face out" & Ted says "I'll have you arrested" & Lou says "It'll be too late, your face will be broken, you're not gonna get too many commercials with a broken face now are you Ted?" & Ted buckles under to force & everybody's happy, except Ted but he's so dumb nobody cares & everybody loves it that Lou's not despondent anymore he's back to his brustling chubby loud love-able whiskey-drinking football-loving ways. Now imagine if Ted were Lou, if Ted were the boss. You know how incredibly fucking brainless Ted is, but let's imagine he understands & is willing to use force. That's the situation we're now in as Americans.

Autopsy Turvy

war gods
bundle up
bright forensic
free radicals
& follow loaners
& coc heads to
have hobbies
& <u>have</u> upheavals
& <u>*have*</u> four volume
histories of the notions
more thoroughly
paste-whydened
yet re-embarked
blasted, subtle,
stupid, failure
of innocence,

the birdcages & handbills bust
they're blood
to be accused
of the universe— mind the blood mind
It is just so, & seems to have
credulity

it is a great annoyance to have so many wishes
loss in the causeways, loss in the clocks
on Mars
most people intend
love's tried open
to form
a puttering quadraphonic blot
it's almost independence day
it's almost time to attempt psychology
the gentle clenched
maw is empty
& made, shuddering

the regulars at the bar
are thrashing Thomas Merton
with checkerboard bathescopes
& babblin about nondiscursive
crap. I am a Times reporter.
I kill people.

                    (Ezra Pound
reading his reader's block
white hair growing down
into the mind of the upturned
muse smelling the musculature
which is being   destroyed

A life is not important
except in the impact it has
on other lives
the invention of new souls
of flame, & of flame
a factor, becoming change
a determining systematic
infinity seams
to be human, to be a sound
of concerns shared therefore really
something that means nothing
but is nonetheless interesting

performed on a rotating stage.
in stereotypical garb, the united
affluent roustabouts are
furnished by concentrated power.
& the guy says to the bartender
but if the trees need a sponsor
shouldn't we simply burn the place
or would that be too subtle.

the sportive hucksters are carping
to the gunshop retirees in the gold dawn
of the unkissed aggregate's nocturnal
comeuppance debut—
a tired astral weakness courts
their senatorial movements
against a black screen
in a bolted flash, a snip
receives a crutch, & question
the radiant clarity
enters the flight information board
& breaks open, dispels
the debauched sovereigns & serial
clemencies, we have earned our
bent burnt things, our tents
& pastries, our violent footnotes
to a future science of mind

as the navigator fell overboard
in the memory of
the roll of flame
the soft regimes
played softly &
even the smallest lie
in its revolutions

mute the bit
circumlocution
agasp & tense
beneath our calm
song of death

Vast crater filled with amazed lighting technicians.

Girls go to college to gain a little knowledge
Boys go to Jupiter to get more stupider

Dissociadelic

—scones of stylistic curios a kind of dance company of
contra-epiphanic recontusion
          withouts the numb summer's
acetate
parsimony burnt
in a stolid banish'd craning placidity's
pre-formatted fête

          Look, he's up in the sky—
gasping & the roof falls in, etc.

an entire ladder company
holds its bladder   America,

It's not magic if you trust it.

the soft night of weasel balls

beeps

o mince pinnacle pillbox beam this
rubber being into
underseeing—

the fins
of the fans
fall all about
the unsevered
ruminants,
like or
not unlike
a carton
  o frye

                              dissolved haste, is dented, is heart
the mademost
              commons stirred, re-unmasked

                    still
        blossom of othered flame,
        still cost, still wilt, still swaying
        the autumnal & sped the swaying
        for the waist & unrepose
        a hover & thought net
        flowerbed of song
        humbling the ravished peril
        the lovmuffins & seagulls
        rousing the spectacle's calm
        repent upwards into the funnel
        where mordant swabs
        houseplant the detailed
        waif, churlish & great.

No Minus

Cocoa Butter

Thoroughly endangered
reticent
                    dinero
dries up in the wellfleet, limpid. Our pissed
center's leafletears jazz &
unadorn the mix up's lugubrious blue bonnet canister
cooked with invariant
etchings of doves crossing the large moon high above an abstractified
blight like
sitting up suddenly in love with the roadway &
talentless, turning to your cup's tin matin, asking
for the shovel, longing
for the smack the
laziest nude laxative volume of Thoreau's
most incompetent pettiness, powerfully,
with appealing adventurous honing kleenex boxes &
shy explosions never before undreamed of, formless, colossal,
anguish, giving, strength,
to the weird fragile matter, shtupping
most of Manhattan & still bored, the linear nondescript
curls of cognitive embarrassment a morass whose
matrix peels junked need from the zookeeper's sock, causing
a riot, causing
the oral traditions

Scapegrace

Lyric, bent,
caught all that
their words are blows
their commas, workaholics
A kin of median excoriance,

The biggest dinosaurs
are crumbling before our eyes,
and many more companies have
serious problems.
the purely bourgeois audience
has lost any sense of its own powerlessness
Ach! a rock she misused
& a hence droopeth, so pistolary the moebius
unconfirmed, your grist's gist
bow down the outvenoms
or any creeping orange flapdragon
(because they steel eggs)
(because they sensate)
(because they spite the jutting parrot-teacher)

but it doesn't really go
does it— America,
(soon to be a boiled pot of Brel)
your beauties tarnish
the reaggravated mesalliant, so kind
so winning
so volubly pertinent, descends into a dolthood
And am I not bound to revere the fate which, thanks to none of
my doing, has brought me here, to the goal of all my wishes?
Let arid nothing running & launched place-name the lip-reason's
taunt,
           mosaic & hashed, the done daily inner discipline of an
           enclosed vehicle on a cabin roadway

courtly society's speculum an angus cauze we fibrillate in ocean
smoked
the raging meth of unchange morphed
nobody marks you, be mocked & wondered at
and look, there is a more admired way of making fountains
   let us sun the net & needle the upset
      if the left wants to redistribute the wealth
   then they need to get really rich
all these gods are a fucking chore man
   indent, recapitulate, blowdry, halt before halting
here in the open-heart washroom
   here in the giddy weapon
here in the capable nose
dadot dot dot, tax & cry, I love you my
litter of hope, let us melt before they do
doused & eternal
true to the paintings and brothers in exile, or turnstile, shrub

   abrupt & lax, moon of conscience, lathe of will
 this summer they wilt, that summer they smolt, inner
& limpid, we
& a wreck, it come from a strobe, the three of cups, hummingbird
     uncombed like rain

Nothing at all Jerry G.

dosed
shimmers, &
the sill forgot to pay for this:
Kick Down! and we'll
keep you informed
Then
the lyric
as experimental possibility
— it's finished
blinking, a psychedelia urnbeing
smashed on the coast of Constitution Day.
Any braids
after urinating bullion
build a portable poured compatriot
to lash to the shuffle &
have, They don't say it's
a fret —
a lazy fuck that would
forever transform four-in-hand
with the heart-of-a-heatless head made
peasantry's organic both/and.
Vitality
in my alembic all-ukelele schtick
a breath sublime
in the parking lot
Lake Placid has survived
complete control (released in mono)
a vertical
                          I do
that doesn't inhale
i.e. is dead
(the bran-muffin
of eternity all-told)
To keep that love

filed,
there:
an immense emotional Buck Owens
blue out of Blake— go &
take every day to every thing
to occupy & divide the parish
synch, the roled sole
source reached
into discontent and landless
impregnated phi beta mateo
the theoretic correct
good middle-class career
against gentry in the mystical
flood of a secret
                    gainsay cinch
in the several lists —
some genial, some action some
slipknot avant sunny I'm
limetreed to take it outta
this linked abyss for borscht
But the most of it ain't
                    noways &
                        our buttons
was a miss-tied reinterpretation
token of community
up in a steady-state layaway . . .

The ends may be folded back
& joined at the centre
which is of course
publicly subsidized

                & flat

[temporomandibular expenses
<u>overdamped</u>
as a percentage covered
at your exadeath]

It is in this then, that
The mist rises from the bourgeois canopy
to reveal Warburton's tome *Philosophy: The Basics*
which is inimitably blurbed by "some
dead motorcyclist's demystified rock star status"
& it can't imagine the lord uploading
that hot mass at half-price without checking
with Doctor Said first. Still,
these savored days, these undisrupted linear progressions
drip back into *silence* &
shield our fisted lean-tos
in the palm of an ad-man's noun-paste
placed like salsa on the back-biter's stylized
latticework for "safe keeping"—
but if the sexist's genius consists of sinister
yet loopy nuisance-building for the corporate
nicety
then how to localize the emotional beach head of our
future's socially engineered fluorescent archetype
in the space of a breadbox or cellblock & not
feel bested by so much cosmic indifference to the neat
package arriving like a technologically predatory kiss
here, in Tahiti, next to the abraided branch of life
I'm nearly beside myself with listlessness. In fact
I am Somehow a Color Macintosh Blowout
doesn't mask the provisionally employed <u>natura</u>
of the cognizant alloy's living down
rebirth inside a dark cave & grooming roots with shards of
decrepit old teacher's manuals; all this that doesn't lend itself
to objectivistcomposition as it has come to be
understood at the undergraduate level in Boise.
But I do love Boise, believe me you

sweat of coloric I would not dull
& dang verboten like a pardner's moose

I'm losing the thread
In the discourse shed
Danville axed
& drowned— it's
pious
croon in replete
impotence—
"Let's turn on the heat
before my pockets swoon" & do
as done unto is drek
or else destiny
dummy.
So much for "clearance"
So much for "irascible"
So much for "homespun"
It looks leniently
entropic, & what Lumpy
wants Lumpy gets,
right Lumpy?

The duration of the spurious peek
of language like a plaster
enfolds now upon its pristine sex
& hardened
cannot not connive Hanover.
We are part of the endless land
& so undive in it, potent
points in the backcountry
homage to marginalization
an inch away
archive moment scan in pain
essential
little hut-wants in vibration.

NO MINUS

after Emptily

keep away the elves they
rethink
& are sowed jitter others of coarse
ad vice as
thousands of three ravens

grow little
quarrels

make a carapace

chased the thought caught
Vimalakirti
& went home
ah   hell
he said to the huntsman

desire misfortune
& there is knowledge

an eloquence, & a cataract

if it is bad junk
support a synthesis
in these jokes
jerked off the road

they found nothing
but a building
it is not wrathful

we need charms

brisket
foists, fails told &
gunk in geographic passion
wrote tumult on a pepper pit
up it went

golly
me again   you again

here again

kerfluffa trees
describe specified biting
as against vernal binding a companion's
compact multi-colored Leibniz-accumulator
the plaster said

perfection
bones

are weak

too easy fatalism lieutenant
lost sound calendar
mad at it
matter
homeostatically regulating

a staunch distant peeping
starvation

they starve

intense limits
extraterrestrial longing
if unacknowledged night
incites implicate persona-lotion

Heaven's net is
filled with cargo others

mostly they smuggle

"if there's a place for those that don't belong
I haven't found it yet"
full in on its face &
the flames they translate
boroughs &

we are very lucky people
in the nineteenth century

were a lot like boards

the self is
faithful to itself
is out of pace with
condiment worship
just nix

emboldened bent's
cleverness virtue

is deep

if we are dumb
wheel the cast shadow
noble one
& say
within the body icelike

reluctant pipe's
suture-speak,

suture-speak, suture-speak

Solidity in angling
secret flour substance
by the rules of syllogisms
gust because
whatever is not a shape

can pace
the abstruse
muse

just counting the thanks
thanks
listen to the lion
home or tone or taupe
we are actually small animals

a little lifetime warranty

at home in   cacophony

the job

aux alouettes: the prose of patrick drevet

not then, light, under cage
presorted lonesome dove undone
splint the middle finger for car trips
like Proust's enigmas of
the annoyable relates to that, but
to pierce the Platonic
butane, black marble, cyan
or else some
plosivity. identikit drama, now
"separation" of looking at
another sheet unstained and lined
dodging?
was it the comet or a misty moon
located in a narrow valley
other gains or losses (attach)
but that was all a dreamshow
antibiotics work best with beer
brute facts what?
no, he needs his rest: sore
w/ you (page 7) Form CRB 818 (4 - 94) etc.
a big hand, please, for the traveling assholes
they keep drawing pictures of it
problems of decipherment, easy to say
zero
an antelope, dried: no raccoons knocking
now pull that drummer out from behind that bottle
speak to the ectoplasm without inhaling
critics tend to see post-war french literature as dominated by
unleavened cake attracted to mis-shapen
falling   in   place
nothing to remember. my phone? my floor?
they droop
we could tape silence and not play it back
birth-mirrors of

elements are uneasy thinking
all three, it turns out
innumerate (missing)

w/ Tom Raworth
4/10/96

ace to &
lazy, just leaving your
skin where you shed it
Buck's mom's dun
shot a sickle-cell elk
as little forms for
forking over the extra
mileage
near or arf?
flecks, thanatose, acid
suffice to recharge,
swish & spit
up the jhodpur diet
wealth of nexus necks
Guy de philosophe funk
drifting undirected
around the potholes
up Annapurna in a legislative
tater
acts of faddish floormat
or abominably
productive
no Beuys nasal stain
speaks tracts laddy
and petty envelopes
w/ windows
lepidoptera for drawn fronds
O trampled lakes of tears
surplanting a megalomaniac's heartburn
(pianissimo)
and don't it make your lost face found

O poor lost glove compartment
who let the pigs
out of their cribs
praise this then
impaling me specifically,
I presume

w/ Tim Davis & Judith Goldman
10/13/96

the job

it's not very ordinary is it
the sky even in observation mingles
unmissed opportunities, fixed
fear at the tongue of things

columns barricade different sites
it is not mine the one wall thrust from a mother
this miser's a broken liquid leapt into a child-man
nine am today heaps light from a varied tongue

it's coarse that way
the clay light on the quit sign
but it can't let me knowing without
all that shit—

plausible calm ringing the body
back but it's busy
in this artificial light you'll have sun, sums, sons
CIA budget secrets & slight trite

peppered with a quiet impatience
I prefer sex
& windowsills to mud books
but not much

for some, labor has lasted up to seventy two hours
minutes envelope the body's upheaval
in the dark grey light from the storm was real light not varied
the road edges the sites the houses

but the unpaid break beaks
& if you're sly the
risk dwindle draws from the singing act a populace convenant
on pavement (it's parallel)

drivers wanted a clad thing
in wrath and music an obstinate continent
buried underground that thing that makes the lights change
while somewhere a woman is in labor or many women the signals

the movement. slight lisp or lip tone. quiet
while I like it garden. collectible oxytocic
oyez. the tending informally— rung tries
runover. sopping city in it, & known.

do you see desire
office murmur
epigram & knucklebone
looming with fingers

but they let it keep waking us or
solve wish.
literalise in clue you.
blast subvocal schmaltz

take it off or take off or take it or
blind not to appraise
to amass
to vow

move comes second to create vatic
trust. sad they make us go away where. a caller.
buy the time to
buy the time.

altered and capable
this if-anything batch
(so laws the usual bound)
sunday balking in that

woman-calling-dog-voice
here in the capital gates announce

the region really
drives articles between

interruptions for words
muddy me— desire

love budgets nothing
love is exceeding its vow

there's no parallel depiction
the road leaps at dusk
the building's windows
that one which is yours

Ma'am.

w/ Jean Donnelly

New Sonnets

The late quartets don't sell so
I kiss your toes & press
callback, natural.
the rumors are flying
through my soft
& shared cousins of
causation the nudge the mourning
the portals cramped & nixed
bleating 2:03 PM
to the potlatch crammed
with books beside the feather.
At the corporate vermin convention
the Kaiser Permanente Bug
is obstructing the governor general's
view of the overhead projector
displaying the petri dish
that they will use to further
the peace process in your town
in your eye in your banana.
Clearly, Ken's fat is more important
than the sensuous possibility I & I
might enjoy. Courage then, my sister,
as the traffic hauls wordplay away
I write an ode to Shakespeare & Co
ending "and everyone & I
stopped reading."
When the idiots legalize their notoriety
the principal teachings return to the people—
pain & stucco shunt the oracle-constructing
roose, it is a given, gravity & desire guide
the bizarre occasions, leap upward troubling
the Oriole fans & driving home into them.
Davidoff, when I see you
blinking — I best

shore up my summery
cousining. My boy's
dead & all that all that
is 100% additive-free,
you see, my friend
the noxious flames
live in me &
into that void
the voice
reports on another particular
which doesn't exist—
— stop me or
save me from such clarity.
it's a pronunciation of stems &
blessings disguise the structure of a multilevel
hierarchical calendar that we believe
was used in pre-Han Escondido—
If kept in allow, cross the need
there, shown up, in a boy's
memories of the rhetoric of undertake
                — works
of bleak risk warden the curved
nestling & store these our cut
toys 'neath rid thoughts
in the paper snap
seeing, snap life.
oblivion is prefigured
in any emotional state.
— ear-soaked & carnal —
a kind of "poet-speak"
pinning nothing to what
we see. saw, shelled, or
simply ignored, friend. . .
it is not that I know
you or want to. It is
rather, that one must distrust
one's distrust as well.

iota of notated craze—
cherry coated—
shock & wire—
racks, mountains, awaited love,
redundancies
color the nothing
cupping the found
frozen
colors, this nothing,
ruined.
Saying is bent against it
& crossed out—
smash the manila Kaiser Permanente bug
let the off-puce one live.
Stalks wind in the ruffian wind.
It may be time to thank all your friends
for the pickles, juts, drinks, & needs.
It may be time to go do that.
The weight of the ringing
earthenware is pretty intense huh.
When you purchase two packs
in the gentle farmer's rain
you get a puttering quadraphonic blot
(no two colossal heads are alike)
but mommy
It doesn't have confidence
It's not alive
(poems about seeing a bear
outside your cabin
don't work for me)
on the bottle it says
no more tears
on Mars
most people intend
love's tried open
to form
crumbles of shot

riddled need
they are soaked fool-trunks
they are drunk with sky
Big Sky, lying
in this night's end
filtered by the fair light
the friends link w/ flame
the ringing & squawking
percussive juts
the flickers, they're annoying
& you're special
no years ago
(infinite elements uncohere)
we do not know
something cloaked in protective
immediacy until the embodied signal beep
abutts covenants of cigaretticism
the cigarette is not a poet &
when we close our eyes
to be false day
there's a lot of groaning
in B.B.F.'s muffled shed
once William Faulkner
called the time & there
was no answer, he felt
trapped in a nondiscursive
frame— the cigarette
is not a sound disbelief but
something that means nothing
like you, like me, like the way
Harry Truman
is totally strange
Two years of the tiger
& some ultra facial moisturizer
fell the obsequious governmental
trash-bin out back of the shiny
cacophony not in Catalonia

It's just another
Debate in Tibetan Buddhist
Education what our relationship
might have been— they stand
there beside the pervasion asking
questions about conches,
colors, & pillars, saying
"I accept it"
"I accept it"
o to be slept
in quit change & cast
there & be kept & give
crossed out
class struggle
with clairvoyance—
the rumors are lying anew—
Anew perfuses the rile.
oblivion is prefigured
in any emotional state.
a kind of "poet-speak"
pinning nothing to what
we see. saw, shelled, or
simply ignored, friend. . .
it is not that I know
you or want to. It is
rather, that one must distrust
cut by it,
autistic haunt-clone in ox-month
it is the risk
the monk who set other people on fire
a mountain of frumpy burnt monks
I say, since I am new, yes
"the frivolous ground"
"verbalized bird diseases in the wind"
this unclean enlightenment tinge
each of us sends a needy victim
The formal constraint

of the unopened flame
the riotous uncatalogued
awful moose
A celestial dragon refraining and frugal
chokes off outlined guck
in Tidewater, Virginia
Dave says "people read biographies
because they want to learn how to be famous"
We cannot exclude the possibility
that a future science of mind
may dispense with the concept
of language in our sense,
but we might as well.
when I call
the violent footnote
there's no answer
in the violent footnote
in the green, fake, waving, treasures' lie
the cauterized eye
is blending its herbal secrets
the sportive hucksters are carping
to the gunshop retirees in the gold dawn
of the unkissed aggregate's nocturnal
comeuppance debut—
a tired astral weakness courts
their senatorial movements
against a black screen
in a bolted flash, a snip
receives a crutch, & question—
we are inert
we are writhing.
A life is not important
except in the impact it has
on other lives
the invention of new souls
of flame, & of flame
a factor, becoming change

a determining systematic
infinity seams the italic dawn
in a series of ritual streaks
gray & rose & real

Love Poems

If you insist long enough
that you're right,
you'll be wrong.

—Hebrew proverb

If a lion could speak, we would not understand him.

—Wittgenstein

Listen to the lion. Like
an owl in the
heaped instant
oil-death craft, my love
my driftwood my
Susquehanna deckhand
disturbance, so sad, printed
into everything taken.
That enormous bandaged
boundary behind
the open muffling
Is to be filled rain
envisioned, tall
fear rim peopled &
transmuting different
bunk in us "surrounding
a little bird-buddha"
in an ad for an ad for
Listen to the lion. Biological
crank turned by burned
sausage into the vacuum
of affirmation where my
oft inner floated mesquite
self's Ismene suddenness
is known spirals sleep and
clear. No roads can show
the middle eye something
other objects shot into
the sky. When giving.
No tactile surface
is stone moist to the
toned raking Paris

you wish. The sun
has several names, like
Sherman, Tazmo, Bonk,
& Harmine— it's risen
raves retake Atlanta
from nothing's lost
laundry room key &
we, clean in those
clothes have regone
there, we've done
a hell of a job.
thank you. We've
done exactly what
was expected of
us. & we
are not dead. 6
tabs re-side baste
& coax ton's opera-knuckle
brisket. Pal 1
is the cloned guy, &
loosely they have
or will have nice
copulated currency, as
if a tusk warranted Suzuki,
as if, portly
a re-stained tore heart's
made timing looked
back in tears over this
strange be.

What you don't know can hurt other people.
                                    —Ted Berrigan

    diopsite earpools
    gone drinkin'
    in the wicked dictionary
    in the gentle
    farmer's rain
    abbreviation'll tinge
    fuschnicken's red arrow
    of perception
    Lisa says
    "stupid,
    but in a useful way"
    poor gummy bear
    lost in the nexus
    of sin
    each wave sends
    psychology
    The lord
    always
    speaks
    as if
    through a tube

> To become unhinged is to admit, finally, the existence of hinges.
> —Kevin Davies

finally, but it's not unfair,
it's mere—
& grows up among
the Norse. Didn't
you tell me
the ricochets
are actually more dangerous. Time
has it's art to play in,
but we don't— whaddya think?
I think it's terrible. Molecular codification
@medlib dot matrix out of loss
to the eyebath brains for breakfast—
keep your head quote
down
unquote — quote
in the secreous noble night
unquote — in the fumbled automatic kin
quote *skin* unquote *again quote But Kevin*
can't afford to have a life to write about &
the europeans are all enormously rich
& very ill. It's a stoned
lower-case roman numeral.
To return to our story. The ensemble
of relations before a tribunal
of light. The light will say because
to speech is like use you amputate.
Juliet, who falls asleep
in a cake. Not only because
we are wrong, but
also because we are
deeply unimpressed. Great Spirit
we run along stars ecstasy curling
clad moments hit cold
as it is
is born

heat most ecstatic
frost groin
in the mild sky all hazed with
joggers. I no longer search for
the unified field but am content
(or feature) am in fact aware
of my own nascent jaundice
(hummingbird crab tacks)
ticks in the cogent
folded but mystic waters never glad confident

know me.

no are what cold

no what sayeth

no the fold yes

wave as it is & where
we must "hold the capitalists accountable"
is there a question?

there is a question.

what heals this?   else
in the end
satisfying stolen nucleus
it's a stoned lower-case
roman numeral &
it's very ill.
it is not yet beautiful enough for
the class of all classes
which are not members of themselves but

to think

the opposites

They say that "home is where the heart is." I think it is where the house is, and the adjacent buildings.
—Emily Dickinson

fact

ouch

the rooms are curtailed mist's dyadic need

The fleet
has unreckoning in it, as Fell's Point
snaps the contract with no-mind

Feel
as sane, & co-rob pundits

you're like Cezanne
you're afraid of being hooked

June's the desk & the pain, Walden, Love Poems, beasts for
slaughter— the gem
at the level of the eye left for NY.
time's
steered nutshell waste places up

gee angel
is the central element
& opts tusk music in this
faulty exhaustion
See also Reciprocity law
paw or paw
the rescue nerve at
the straight chip away solvent

boast of unnoticed

clammer's tense

a shut rain in a nutshell toward.

the inner fire's grate

I'm not going to tell you anything.
                              —Jasper Johns

    The rage of they taints incorporate Buddhahood's jipped fixation. Any nascent craze is upped and close— we're all roses, we're all crates. On the last day the unwilling Mind lingers amidst a ream of chisel excess. The glowing kosmoi of betrayal's unreal— only grass stacked like Scriptures mask the faults & poses. The crowds vanish— globular & cunning, the charismatic *known* plunging bouts past this curt administrative satisfaction-device burnt in the caucus of . . . Still, there are no questions in the sawed-off foe-self lurch we align & reduct as shimmered pentance builds it is not unbound flux but intrinsic gentle showering the sudden torn up resentment written on a flowing stream to you my love—It's the heart's use as utterance till, a jade count on the bliss wall, playing chemistry, playing this body of want's tacit strain as detailed unguent *comes* the lost kinematic fricassee of woo torn from the chaste air's bit-person vision to un-be in this spurious treatise whose pert lunacy is patibility & plainly to our betterment's trance-moor groaning. A steep vocabulary within love's other nothing, a basis unserving to hold felt night, brisk & gone, lost there in meaning, our caustic need unraveled, turning the shreds to thoughts.

To keep the mixtures ("revealed")
chip clip — a life of checks

      endorsed before canceled & do does
Actually place things out in front of me

the role of the pinafore is to protect
yes
no specific title mentioned
for it is cold
        luck
        & the brooding
        mercenary definitions

one's own soul

time

self conception

sleep etc.   if you try
surviving
not really stopping
or else stopping

I don't know but I don't think the phrase
"stay in touch" should be used
quite so lightly.

"People know what they do, most people even know why they do
what they do, but what they don't know is what they do does."

           —Foucault

 on film
what solitude very obviously does

can tell about
    can choose, & reacquaint

                    Philosophical conclusions
should not surprise us. Their halos

are causations— yet we cannot be seen
even in the midst of

as it is
is weathering, a kind of width
with speech.
           mercenary definitions

clear
the nut's above &
above the nuts, thee, Lysistratan islands locked in the
knave pastoral tentpost

piles of tops clasped by the chromium beholden— rested
mince, corporeal, cruxed, bi-fed, lovely, just stunning

    ocean
    as she held her shirt-tail in her teeth
    Glenlivet
    The Music of Morton Feldman

I've yet to see a dungeon.
like someone.

On Weathering

for John Cage

Skin II, 1973

flux nub, a
"kit of parts" the blades balance
glued together as a neutralizing
stylistic obscenity— beached urn to generate have witnessed
the fragmentation of the cyberspace metaphor, untold
in tacit town, astonishing ether: a relative, freedom

the sentence that evinced that
acetate

cuddled up with the lab's godfather

Flags II, 1967-70

artificially rusticated preoccupation
"dressed smooth" for
The counterpart of the kiss of death is the war of convenience
The counterpart of the
hard & closed building box soft & taught
in sloped sealants but the face of each unfinished form
you lay fills the white circus flame
that, immersed, tumbles to
show up in the "put on" that "hits you back"

our existence are beautiful
fills or creates space
they decide what time is it is serving & precise

Flag on Orange Field

Sometime around 1970 the role of the avant garde began to change from that of being ahead of the pack to that of laughing at anybody that thought they knew what they were talking about.

The Critic Sees, 1962

sculpmetal, 1 3/8 x 7 3/4 x 1 1/2,
Collection the artist

But we have seen
the object known

like the animal in Kafka
from the outset (gems
to be eaten & ontologically disguised
Man-in-the-Moon Marigolds
breath of
a widow's bitter dignity
the self-cause stack of old *New Yorkers*
during Mardi Gras, parathyroid requiredness
in space-time a choice foundation
(Utah *at* Wyoming) the glass tip tips
please see I am reflected on
insect migration
in a society which is wholly alienated

Jubilee

shingle to us shines live tusks taste like dope. the president
is free to separate or soften frenzy. outthink to the tumult
        is vivid when swimming imprint stuns Raphael
        Leonidas Trujillo, a seaport in NW Peru, *vireo*
        I should go, the downward

        scraping of a ruler

Between the Clock & the Bed, 1984

The June 1st is only hops again the next present in the seven
layers of the aura. In order to be a reason the reason must
be experienced. The reason was experienced.
mad staggers & macebearers. Rock talks
up clock to tell
& is told it tells

Untitled, 1977

<u>dialectique</u>
yeah right
upper undone lonesome Espy Award
the lack
holds the mirror up
not as a thought
thought
(which erases cataleptic specialties)
the past by making all
is <u>alone</u> for reasons on their
life's ups

Dancers on a Plane, 1982

to nurture oozing dissolution
is vivid when stopping

Merce
with a clean cloth
coughs

Amino
I mean
oh, take at least 1000 mg of
C
embracing
new ideas
and invoking
vital force

Tracing, 1978

I am swimming and I melt
makes me happy
Duchamp's Bride
removed from consciousness
by a cubist midlife crisis
or the Catholic Church

presentations
look to be avoided

Untitled, 1988

the critic between being and self-help
while the bookseller goes to the volume

this time using
as a source
in the absolute I
"irritate him,"
etc.

Perilous Night, 1982

Exhibited only in Washington

John
didn't say
as soon as Genet in
the body's way
of getting rid of toxins

a daunted laughter's self-image
of self-healing questions for each
subluxation's vital doubt

dusk of the imprint
of the artist's right

thanks that light
& returns it.

Study for Racing Thoughts, 1983

a nonphysical healing of
Leo Castelli
During a Valentine's Day flight from
the devil in Dr. Albright's old boyfriend

red clover, powdered,
Collection the artist
to the being of the Other
Prom Night

~~This was our paradox: no course of~~
~~action could be determined by a rule, because~~
~~every course of action can be made to accord with the rule.~~

Summer, 1985

<u>Minotaur Moving His House</u>

Home Improvement
to a fault

tied on the autobiographical back
and in a priori anguish
the self-cause stack
is vivid when stopping

the cafe remainders the circle as <u>meaning</u>
<u>revealing nothing manifested</u>
by a particular New York

Al takes his latest romance a little too seriously. We are being
threatened
by the bloodiest and most stupid of wars.

Between the Clock and the Bed, 1982

they know how to talk. they linger against a rough surface in washing the act of solving

From False Start, 1960

doubtless it happens
<u>determining</u>
nothing
before it
loves
the unique

Tracing, 1977

untitled body's
rid in the absolute
returns   to a fault
as a source for each

Recent & Select
ROOF BOOKS

ROOF BOOKS
are published by
Segue Foundation, 300 Bowery, New York, NY 10012
Sor a complete listing of books please visit our website at **segue.org**

Roof Books are distributed by
SMALL PRESS DISTRIBUTION
1341 Seventh Avenue, Berkeley, CA. 94710-1403.
Phone orders: 800-869-7553
spdbooks.org